Published by The Child's World®
1980 Lookout Drive • Mankato, MN 56003-1705
800-599-READ • www.childsworld.com

Photographs ©: Shutterstock Images, cover, 1, 10, 18, 21; Sarawut Kundej/Shutterstock Images, 5; Francisco J Ramos Gallego/Shutterstock Images, 6, 24; Sven Hansche/Shutterstock Images, 9; GSFC/LaRC/JPL, MISR Team/NASA, 13; Val Iva/Shutterstock Images, 14; Ethan Daniels/Shutterstock Images, 17

Copyright © 2022 by The Child's World®
All rights reserved. No part of this book may be reproduced or utilized in any form or by any means without written permission from the publisher.

ISBN 9781503850071 (Reinforced Library Binding)
ISBN 9781503850460 (Portable Document Format)
ISBN 9781503851221 (Online Multi-user eBook)
LCCN 2021939908

Printed in the United States of America

ABOUT THE AUTHOR

Emma Huddleston lives in Minnesota with her husband. She enjoys running, swing dancing, and writing books for young readers.

CHAPTER ONE
Busy and Bright ...4

CHAPTER TWO
Diverse Reefs ...11

CHAPTER THREE
Life without Corals ...16

GLOSSARY ...22
TO LEARN MORE ...23
INDEX ...24

Busy and Bright

Yellow, blue, and purple fish swim by. Sea turtles glide through the ocean. Corals cover parts of the floor below. They look like brightly colored plants. But corals are animals. Small fish dart between them. Some are looking for food in the corals.

Many types of plants and animals call coral reefs home.

Corals come in many shapes, sizes, and colors. Brain corals get their name from their shape.

Corals are important in their **ecosystem**. An individual coral is also called a polyp. Most polyps are less than .5 inches (1.5 cm) wide, but there are many types of corals. The mushroom coral has large polyps. They are about 5 inches (12.7 cm) wide.

Polyps connect their **exoskeletons** together. They form groups called colonies. Colonies can be the size of a small car. Many colonies form a reef. Coral reefs are **habitats** made of many types of polyps.

FUN FACT

More than 6,000 **species** of coral exist.

Many corals get their color from algae. These corals are red, green, and brown. Algae are plantlike **organisms**. They grow in the corals. Corals and algae work together to survive. The corals give the algae a place to live. The algae get food from the corals' waste. In return, the algae help make food for corals. Corals can grow ten times faster with algae than without. Their partnership helps build bigger reefs. Bigger reefs support more wildlife.

Busy and bright ecosystems form because of corals. Corals are homes for some fish and plants. They are a food source for others. Many plants and people depend on corals to survive.

Algae on corals are called zooxanthellae (zoh-uh-zan-THEL-ee).

The Belize Barrier Reef is the second largest coral reef in the world. Many people from around the world travel to see it.

Diverse Reefs

Most corals live in warm, shallow water. The Belize Barrier Reef is in the Caribbean Sea. But some corals can grow in deeper, colder places. Corals can grow separately there. They do not always form reefs.

Both coral reefs and rain forests have a lot of different animals. Coral reefs are sometimes called rain forests of the sea.

The largest coral reef is the Great Barrier Reef. It is off the coast of Australia. It covers 1,430 miles (2,300 km). More than 9,000 species of plants and animals live there. Scientists are still discovering more. More than 1.6 million people visit it every year.

Coral reefs cover less than 1 percent of the ocean. But they are one of the most **diverse** ecosystems in the world. Millions of plants and animals live in them. They offer safe shelter. Algae, crabs, and shrimp live among corals. Fish, sea snakes, dolphins, and sharks also live in coral reefs.

Australia's Great Barrier Reef is so large it can be seen from space.

Why We Need Coral Reefs

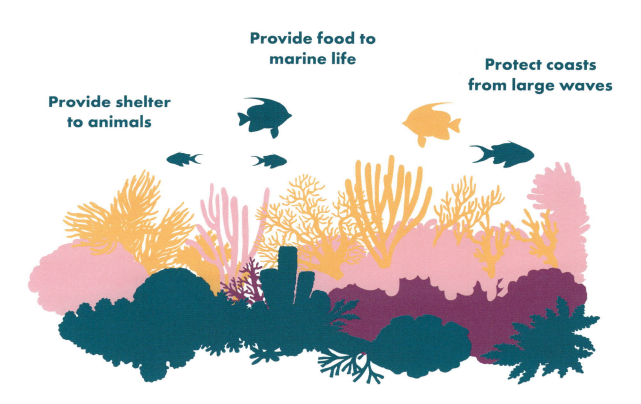

Provide shelter to animals

Provide food to marine life

Protect coasts from large waves

Corals have many important roles. Animals use them to find protection, shelter, and food.

Corals have many roles in their ecosystems. Fish live, mate, and hide from **predators** in corals. Young fish stay there before going into open waters. This keeps them safe. Corals are also a food source. Some fish, worms, snails, and sea stars eat them. Many creatures in the ocean depend on healthy coral reefs to live. Corals protect coasts as well. Corals are a barrier between big waves and land. They help lessen storm damage.

Life without Corals

Corals face many threats. Rising ocean temperatures are stressful for them. Warm water can cause algae to become dangerous to corals. This causes bleaching. Bleaching is when corals get rid of their algae partners. They turn white. Bleaching weakens corals. They are at a higher risk for disease and death.

Corals go through bleaching when their algae become dangerous. Corals without their algae may die.

Without healthy coral reefs, many animals would lose their homes and food sources.

Without corals, many species would not have a place to live. Those animals could die off forever. Ecosystems would lose diversity. More than 500 million people rely on food from reefs. Many others make money from travelers who visit reefs.

FUN FACT
Scientists use corals to make some medicines.

Corals are important for many reasons. People and governments are trying to protect them. People study reefs and the threats they face. They try to find ways to help corals recover from bleaching. Governments create marine parks. The parks are protected areas for corals and all wildlife.

Scientists want to protect reefs. They grow corals. Then, they add the corals to a damaged reef.

diverse (di-VURS) Being diverse means to have many different kinds of something. Coral reefs are diverse habitats where many plants and animals live.

ecosystem (EE-koh-siss-tuhm) An ecosystem is all of the living and nonliving things in an area. Corals play an important role in an ecosystem.

exoskeletons (ek-soh-SKEL-ih-tons) Exoskeletons are hard, bony parts on the outside of the body. Corals grow hard exoskeletons.

habitats (HAB-uh-tatz) Habitats are places with the right temperature, weather, food, and water for an animal to live. Coral reefs are habitats for many kinds of fish.

organisms (OR-guh-nih-zuhms) Organisms are individual living things, such as plants or animals. Coral reefs are home to many organisms.

predators (PRED-uh-turs) Predators are animals that hunt and eat other animals. Corals offer shelter for small fish hiding from predators.

species (SPEE-sheez) A species is a specific group of animals that has the same features. Thousands of coral species exist.

BOOKS

Hulick, Kathryn. *Coral Reefs*. New York, NY: AV2 by Weigl, 2019.

London, Martha. *Looking Into the Ocean*. Mankato, MN: The Child's World, 2020.

Schuetz, Kari. *Life in a Coral Reef*. Minneapolis, MN: Bellwether Media, 2016.

WEBSITES

Visit our website for links about corals:
childsworld.com/links

Note to Parents, Teachers, and Librarians: We routinely verify our Web links to make sure they are safe and active sites. So encourage your readers to check them out!

INDEX

algae, 8, 12, 16

Belize Barrier Reef, 11
bleaching, 16, 20

Caribbean Sea, 11
colonies, 7

ecosystem, 7–8, 12, 15, 19
exoskeletons, 7

Great Barrier Reef, 12

mushroom coral, 7

organisms, 8

polyp, 7
predators, 15

reefs, 7–8, 11–12, 14, 15, 19–20